TABLE OF CONT]

Chapter 1
Baptism   *Page 1*

Administered by immersion into water, or the pouring of water, accompanied by the words, "I baptize you in the name of the Father, and of the Son and of the Holy Spirit." (Mt.28:)

Chapter 2
Confirmation   *Page 10*

Administered by the laying on of hands, the anointing with Holy Chrism and the words, "Be sealed with the gift of the Holy Spirit." The ordinary minister of Confirmation in the Latin Church is the bishop. A priest can confirm an adult at his/her Baptism or Profession of Faith and can confirm anyone in danger of death.

Chapter 3
Holy Eucharist   *Page 19*

The bread and wine become the Body, Blood, Soul and Divinity of Jesus (called the Real Presence) during the Eucharistic Prayer said by the priest (or bishop) at Mass. The consecrated bread and wine can be distributed by Extraordinary Ministers.

Chapter 4
Reconciliation   *Page 34*

Reconciliation is the sacrament by which Jesus, through His Church, forgives sins, which are committed after Baptism. The sacrament is sometimes called Confession because it usually requires the confessing of sins to a priest. (In extraordinary circumstances, Reconciliation can occur without prior confession.)

Chapter 5
Anointing of the Sick   *Page 48*

The Anointing of the Sick is administered by a priest who anoints the person's forehead and hands with oil saying, "Through this holy anointing, may the Lord in His love and mercy, help you with the gift of the Holy Spirit" and "May God who frees you from sin, save you and raise you up." This anointing forgives sins, often heals, and, at times, prepares the person to accept death.

Chapter 6
Matrimony   *Page 56*

Matrimony is administered by the vows made publicly by the two spouses. The sacrament bestows special helps to the couple to fulfill this lifelong commitment to God and to each other. Church law also requires the presence of a priest and two witnesses (unless special circumstances preclude this possibility, or a dispensation has been obtained).

Chapter 7
Holy Orders   *Page 70*

Holy Orders is administered by the bishop through the laying on of hands. Through this sacrament, a man becomes a priest and shares in all the powers intended by Christ, especially the power to forgive sins, consecrate the Eucharist, anoint the sick and, at times, to confirm. Holy Orders is also the basis for sharing in the teaching authority of the Church.

INTRODUCTION

THE KINGDOM OF GOD

1. Catholic Sacraments can only be explained fully in light of God's kingdom made available to us through Jesus.

2. Two thousand years ago, the Word became flesh and made His dwelling among us. (Jn. 1:14)

3. Thirty years later, Jesus said, "The kingdom of God is at hand". (Mk.1:15) "Come away and proclaim the kingdom of God." (Lk. 9:60)

4. Jesus gave Himself fully to this work of the kingdom, which was accompanied by divine signs, "Jesus taught in their synagogues, proclaimed the good news of the kingdom and cured the people of every disease and illness." (Mt.4:23)

5. Jesus enlisted others to help with this task. He told His disciples. "It has pleased your Father to give you the kingdom." (Lk.12:32)

6. Jesus even entrusted to Peter, "The keys of the kingdom of heaven." (Mt. 16:19)

7. After Jesus' death and resurrection, the disciples understood clearly that the Kingdom of God had

I

broken through into human history. Paul writes, "God has given us the wisdom to understand fully the mystery." (Eph.1:9)

8. The Risen Jesus Himself is the Kingdom of God. "It pleased God to make absolute fullness reside in Him." (Col.1:19)

9. Peter explained this great mystery to the people on Pentecost. "God has made both Lord and Messiah this Jesus whom you crucified." (Acts2:36)

10. Everyone can enter Jesus' kingdom by believing in Jesus and by being baptized (as will be explained in the chapter on the Sacrament of Baptism).

11. After Baptism, Jesus has provided other sacraments so that God's kingdom increases within the baptized believer.

12. Therefore, Jesus' kingdom has two parts:
    a) an inner life of faith which is God's life within the believer
    b) external rites called sacraments which begin and strengthen that divine life within

II

CHAPTER 1

BAPTISM

Definition

Baptism is the sacrament in which someone who believes in Jesus receives the Holy Spirit, who removes all sins (both original and personal), and makes the believer a child of God and heir to Jesus' kingdom.

Besides the sacrament of water Baptism, the Church teaches two other forms:

a) Baptism of Desire, which is received by someone who believes in Jesus but has not been able to receive water Baptism (such as a catechumen).

b) Baptism of Blood, which is received by someone who sacrifices their life for the sake of Jesus' kingdom.

OLD TESTAMENT

1. The words "Baptism" and "to baptize" do not appear in the Old Testament.

2. Although the Old Testament does not use the word Baptism, Judaism did have a purification rite, which was used to admit Gentiles into the Jewish religion.

3. The Catholic Baptismal ceremony, mentions many Old Testament events which speak prophetically of Jesus' gift of sacramental Baptism.

1

a) the Spirit breathing on the waters (Gen. C1:2)
b) God saving Noah in the ark (Gen. C7)
c) Moses leading the Israelites through the Red Sea (Ex. C.15)
d) Joshua's crossing of the Jordan River to claim the Promised Land (Jos. C3)

NEW TESTAMENT

John's Baptism comes to the foreground

4. All four gospels speak of John baptizing in the Jordan River.

5. John's baptizing is not limited to Gentiles who wanted to become Jews but everyone, Jews and Gentiles, were invited to receive his Baptism.

6. Mark writes, "All the Judean countryside and the people of Jerusalem went out in great numbers. They were being baptized by him in the Jordan River as they confessed their sins" (1:5). (This text is obviously the basis for Mt.3: 5-6 and Lk.3:3.)

7. All four gospels contrast the Baptism of John with the Baptism of Jesus. John's Baptism is of water. Jesus' Baptism is with the Holy Spirit and fire. (Mt.3:11, Mk1:8, Lk3:16 and Jn1:34) These texts show clearly the greater divine power of Jesus' Baptism.

8. John's Baptism prefigured and prepared for the more powerful Baptism of Jesus. John constantly

proclaimed, "One more powerful than I is to come after me" (Mk1:7 also Mt3:11 and Lk 3:16).

9. The extensive reporting on John's ministry by all four gospels witnesses to the great importance John had in preparing the way for Jesus'.

10. It is certain that John's Baptism was a passing phenomenon giving way to Jesus' Baptism, which has been administered for two thousand years. This is shown by an event at Ephesus. St. Paul discovered some disciples of John at Ephesus who knew and received only "the Baptism of John." He instructed them in the Baptism of Jesus and then baptized them (Acts 19:1-7).

BAPTISM OF JESUS

11. The New Testament provides extensive teaching on the importance and effects of Jesus' Baptism.

After the Resurrection

12. After Jesus rose from the dead, "he showed them (the apostles) in many convincing ways that he was alive, appearing to them over the course of forty days and speaking about the reign of God" (Acts 1:3).

13. Besides convincing the apostles that He had truly risen, Jesus gave them the Great Commission, their task for the rest of their lives. "Go, therefore, and

make disciples of all the nations. Baptize them in the name of the Father, and of the Son and of the Holy Spirit" (Mt.28:19).

14. Jesus promised salvation to those who obey His command to be baptized. "The man who believes in it and accepts Baptism will be saved" (Mk.16:16).

15. Jesus also spoke of condemnation to those who refuse, "The man who refuses to believe in it will be condemned" (Mk.16:16).

Acts of the Apostles

16. The Acts of the Apostles describes clearly that the apostles fulfilled this Great Commission, preaching everywhere and baptizing all who believed. The following texts show that Baptism was the central gift for those who believed the message.

a) <u>Those who heard Peter on Pentecost Day</u>: "Those who accepted his message were baptized, some three thousand were added that day". (2:41)

b) <u>Samaritans who believed the preaching of Philip</u>: "men and women both accepted Baptism." (8:12)

c) <u>The Eunuch to whom Philip explained the Scripture</u>: "Philip went down into the water with the Eunuch and baptized him." (8:38).

d) <u>Cornelius and his Gentile family after hearing Peter preach:</u> "So he (Peter) gave orders that they be baptized in the name of Jesus Christ" (10:48).

4

e) Saul after meeting the Risen Jesus on the road to Damascus was baptized by Ananias "He got up and was baptized..." (9:18).

f) <u>Lydia from Thyatira</u> after hearing Paul's preaching "she and her household had been baptized." (16:15).

g) <u>The jailer and his family</u> when Paul preached to them after the earthquake shook the jail. "At that late hour of the night he took them (Paul and Silas) in and bathed their wounds: then he and his whole household were baptized" (16:33).

h) <u>The Corinthians after hearing Paul:</u> "Many of the Corinthians, too, who heard Paul believed and were baptized" (18:8).

17. The Acts of the Apostles gives a picture of the early Church's missionary activity. Baptism is the clear door into Christ's Kingdom.

St. Paul's Teaching

18. Paul's New Testament letters provide extensive teaching on Baptism.

19. Baptism unites all believers under Jesus in a common faith. "There is one Lord, one faith, one Baptism, one God and Father of all." (Eph.4:5)

20. By Baptism, the believer really enters into the death and rising of Jesus. "Through Baptism into his death, we were buried with Him." (Rom.6:4) "If we

have been united with Him through likeness to his death, so shall we be through a like resurrection." (Rom.6:5, Col:2:12)

21. Baptism bestows the Holy Spirit:
"It was in one Spirit that all of us, whether Jew or Greek, slave or free, were baptized unto one body." All of us have been given to drink of the one Spirit (1Cor.12:13).

22. Baptism makes us children of God.
"Each one of you is a son of God because of your faith in Christ Jesus. All of you who have been baptized into Christ have clothed yourselves with Him." (Gal.3:26-27)

NECESSITY OF BAPTISM

23. Those who saw the Easter visions did not need to be baptized, because Jesus Himself bestowed the Holy Spirit directly.

24. For those who came later, Jesus had another plan to bestow the Holy Spirit, namely, that those who believed would tell others. These others, by believing this good news and by being baptized, would receive the Holy Spirit. (1Pt.3:21)

THE EFFECTS OF BAPTISM

25. Based upon all of these New Testament texts, the Catholic Church teaches that the believer, by Baptism:
    a) receives forgiveness of all sins. This includes

b) both original sin and all sins committed by the believer before Baptism.

c) receives forgiveness of all punishment due to pre-Baptismal sins.

d) becomes:

    1) an adopted child of God

    2) a sharer in God's nature

    3) a temple of the Holy Spirit

    4) a recipient of infused powers of faith, hope, charity, and the sanctifying and charismatic gifts of the Holy Spirit

26. The believer is incorporated into the Body of Christ, the Church, receiving both a relationship to God and to all the other baptized.

27. The believer receives an indelible spiritual mark. This is called the spiritual character of Baptism. (Confirmation and Holy Orders also bestow a similar gift.) Because of this gift, Baptism needs to be received only once. This baptismal seal consecrates the person to participate in liturgical worship, to receive the other sacraments, and to witness to all concerning the riches available in Christ Jesus.

28. The goal of all Christian life is to remain faithful to this baptismal seal until death.

The Ultimate Goal – Heaven

29. By receiving the Holy Spirit in Baptism, the believer can directly experience God in heaven. Catholic theology calls this gift the Beatific Vision.

RESPONSIBILITIES OF THE BAPTIZED

30. An adult who receives Baptism accepts Jesus as his/her Lord and must have a committal to follow Jesus and live according to the new way of His kingdom.

31. A complete picture of Christian responsibilities can only be gained by a constant reading of the Bible, especially the New Testament, and by following the teaching of the Catholic Church.

32. The power to live up to the baptismal responsibilities comes only from the Holy Spirit, who is already given to the baptized. "All who are led by the Spirit of God are sons of God". (Rom.8:14)

33. Accepting Baptism requires a radical and total commitment to God's kingdom. Unfortunately, too many of the baptized have no idea of their responsibilities.

Infant Baptism

34. In the case of infant Baptism, the responsibility rests primarily upon the adults who present their child for Baptism.

35. Unfortunately, while Baptism can be seen as an important ceremony that certainly should be done, adults can overlook the important obligations toward the baptized infant.

36. The primary obligation is that the parents themselves be faithful members of the Church, participating fully in Church life and attending mass every Sunday.

37. The parents must also provide the full Catholic education and formation. Because the infant did not go through the conversion process and personal choice of an adult who chooses Baptism, the child must be provided every opportunity for a Catholic upbringing Therefore, these must be made up in the years ahead.

38. Parents should think of a full Catholic education, within a Catholic school. Too often, secular priorities and concerns lead parents to send their children to public schools when Catholic education is available.

39. Getting their child baptized is frequently God's fresh invitation for parents to return to, or to deepen, their Church practice. They now have extra reasons to be more faithful to religious duties.

CHAPTER 2

CONFIRMATION

(My thanks to the excellent article in the Catholic Encyclopedia by P. T. Camelot.)

Definition

Confirmation is the sacrament by which a baptized person receives a greater incorporation into the Holy Spirit and the Church.

Relationship to Baptism

1. Confirmation is so closely linked to Baptism that Eastern Churches have this anointing take place immediately after Baptism is administered.

2. In the West, adult converts to the Catholic Church also receive Confirmation at the same time as their Baptism or Profession into the Church.

3. Therefore, only in the West and usually only in cases of infant Baptism, are the two sacraments of Baptism and Confirmation separated by a number of years.

OLD TESTAMENT PROPHECIES

4. Isaiah prophesied concerning the Messiah. "The Spirit of the Lord shall rest upon him." (11:2)

5. Ezekiel promised God's Spirit for a new Israel. "I will give you a new heart and place a new Spirit within you." (36:26)

6. Joel prophesied that this Holy Spirit upon the Messiah would be given to all the people. "Then afterward I will pour out my Spirit upon all mankind." (Joel 3:1)

The Gospel Picture

7. It might seem strange, but Jesus' Baptism is the gospel model for our Confirmation.

8. When John the Baptist saw the Spirit descend, he was able to testify clearly that Jesus "is God's Chosen One". (1:34)

9. Jesus often promised an outpouring of the Holy Spirit. "From within him rivers of living water shall flow." (Here He was referring to the Spirit whom those that came to believe in Him were to receive.) (Jn.7:38-39)
    "If I go, I will send Him (the Paraclete) to you." (Jn.16:7)

New Testament Picture of
the Early Church

10. The Early Church had two classes of believers, those who saw the Risen Jesus and those who believed in Jesus through the preaching of eyewitnesses.

Confirmation

11. For those who saw the Risen Jesus, scripture records special moments for their unique receiving of the Holy Spirit, given to them for their worldwide mission.

Disciples Receiving the Spirit

12. The Risen Jesus appeared to the disciples on Easter Sunday night: "Then he breathed on them and said: 'Receive the Holy Spirit. If you forgive men's sins, they are forgiven them; if you hold them bound, they are held bound'" (Jn.20:22-23). This text is often called "John's Pentecost".

13. Another scriptural picture comes from Luke in his Acts of the Apostles.
    a) Jesus told the apostles not to begin preaching until they received the special anointing of the Holy Spirit. "You will receive power when the Holy Spirit comes down on you; then you are to be my witnesses" (1:8).
    b) This promised coming of the Holy Spirit happened on "the day of Pentecost": "All were filled with the Holy Spirit. They began to express themselves in foreign tongues and make bold proclamations as the Spirit prompted them" (2:4).

14. Comparing John with Luke shows that John associates the Holy Spirit with the forgiveness of sins, while Luke (in the Acts) focuses on praying in tongues and bold proclamation.

15. Obviously, the disciples' initiation into the Kingdom is unique and not necessarily a model for everyone.

NEW TESTAMENT PICTURE OF OTHER BELIEVERS

16. The New Testament shows the great concern of the Early Church for a full initiation of all new believers who had not seen Jesus.

17. Very important, therefore, are two texts in the Acts of the Apostles in which already baptized believers are prayed with for a second anointing of the Holy Spirit.

18. After Philip had preached and conferred Baptism upon new believers in Samaria, Peter and John are sent. These two "prayed that they (new believers) might receive the Holy Spirit. It had not as yet come down upon any of them since they had only been baptized in the name of the Lord Jesus" (8: 15-16).

19. In Ephesus, Paul finds some disciples who have received John's Baptism but had never even heard of the Holy Spirit. After explaining about Jesus who sends the Holy Spirit, Paul baptizes them in the name of the Lord Jesus (19:5). Then, "as Paul laid his hands on them, the Holy Spirit came down on them and they began to speak in tongues and to utter prophecies" (19:6).

20. These two texts show believers experiencing a second receiving of the Holy Spirit after their Baptism.

21. A special witness to this unique sending of the Holy Spirit by the laying on of hands is, strangely enough, Simon the magician who sees the Holy Spirit's wonders and wants to buy the powers from Peter, "Give me that power, too, so that if I place my hands on anyone he will receive the Holy Spirit" (8:19).

22. These two texts in the Acts of the Apostles also show the need for the person laying hands to have a special office (e.g., Peter, John and Paul).

23. This linking of Baptism and the subsequent laying on of hands is clear in Hebrews 6:1. "Let us, then, go beyond the initial teaching about Christ and about baptisms and laying on of hands".

24. In the thirteenth century, the great St. Thomas Aquinas taught that the visible manifestation of the Holy Spirit upon Jesus in the Jordan was the model for the Christian receiving the plentitude of the Spirit.

CHURCH HISTORY

25. In the early centuries, Confirmation generally comprised one single ceremony with Baptism, forming a "double sacrament" (the words of St. Cyprian, Bishop of Carthage).

26. With the multiplication of infant Baptisms throughout the year and the increase of rural parishes, it became impossible for the bishop to baptize everyone (as had been done in the beginning).

27. In the Western Church, the strong desire to have the bishop complete the Baptism, led to the separation of the two sacraments.

28. At one point, a double anointing took place. As the newly baptized came out of the baptismal immersion, first the priest and secondly the bishop anointed the person. This first anointing by the priest remains attached to the baptismal sacrament when it is not followed immediately by Confirmation.

29. From the third century on, a second rite of laying on of hands that completes the sacrament of Baptism is clearly attested to by Christian writers.

30. Cyprian, the bishop of Carthage, writes about the baptized being presented to the "leaders of the Church" so that "by our prayers and by the imposition of hands, they may receive the Holy Spirit and be perfected by the seal of the Lord (Epist 73.9-Pl 3:1160).

31. In the third century, because the bishop baptized most new believers, water Baptism and the laying on of hands with anointing of oil were usually joined in the same rite.

32. In other cases, such as emergency Baptism or Baptism by priests in rural areas, the bishop would

complete these Baptisms by the second rite of laying on of hands.

33. By the fifth century, Pope Innocent I recalled that this completion of sacramental Baptism was reserved to bishops and distinguished Confirmation from the regular anointing given by all priests at Baptism.

34. Since then, the two sacraments have been clearly distinguished in the Western Church.

ACTUAL BESTOWAL OF THE SACRAMENT

35. The New Testament texts stress the laying on of hands to impart the Holy Spirit.

36. Very early, perfumed oil (chrism) was added, highlighting the name Christian, which means "anointed".

Necessity

37. Confirmation is not absolutely necessary for salvation. However, as part of the initiation rites, the believer must not neglect receiving this sacrament.

Effects

38. Because Baptism and Confirmation are so clearly linked, a true doctrinal dilemma exists. One theology might limit Baptism too much to make sure that Confirmation has clear effects. Another theology

might exalt Baptism so much that Confirmation is called into question.

39. The clearest explanation is to see Confirmation as an increase and a deepening of baptismal grace.

40. There are five clear effects:
    a) a power to call God Father "Abba"
    b) a power to experience Jesus as Lord and Savior
    c) a greater control of the Holy Spirit through His gifts
    d) a greater bonding with the Church
    e) greater strength to evangelize and to undergo sufferings while confessing Jesus as Lord

THE CHURCH FULLY ALIVE!

41. By Confirmation, the Church proclaims and acts in bold faith that the baptismal grace should claim the believer's entire being (sanctifying gifts).

42. Unfortunately, the Church has not boldly proclaimed the important role of religious experiences in releasing fully this Confirmation anointing.

43. Also, the absence of charismatic gifts in the Eucharistic assembly and the widespread ignorance of charisms in the Catholic community violate St. Paul's clear admonitions in 1 Corinthians:

Confirmation

a) "Now, brothers, I do not want to leave you in ignorance about spiritual gifts." (12:1)
b) "Set your hearts on spiritual gifts - above all, the gift of prophecy." (14:1)
c) "I should like it if all of you spoke in tongues." (14:5)
d) "Set your hearts on prophecy." (14:39)
e) "... do not forbid those who speak in tongues" (14:39).

44. Confirmation, therefore, is extremely important, bestowing upon the believer vast powers of the Holy Spirit which should be released, at various times, throughout the person's lifetime.

45. As the Church fully understands and preaches the actions of the Holy Spirit, then Confirmation's effects will be evident and the Holy Spirit will no longer be "the forgotten Person of the Trinity".

CHAPTER 3

THE EUCHARIST

Definition

The Eucharist is a sacrament in which a baptized person receives the body and blood, soul and divinity of Jesus Christ under the species of bread and wine.

1. The Eucharist is both sacrifice and sacrament.

1. As a sacrifice, at all times, in every part of the world, the Eucharist reenacts every day the death of Jesus, obtaining the heavenly Father's blessings upon the whole world.

3. As a sacrament, the Eucharist has two aspects:

    a) the Real Presence of Jesus under the appearance of bread and wine

    b) the receiving of Holy Communion by believers

4. This booklet, focusing on the seven sacraments, will treat of the Eucharist as sacrament and will not explain the Eucharist as sacrifice.

Preparing For the Eucharist (Old Testament)

5. The Eucharist as a holy meal is foreshadowed by the Jewish concept of hospitality around the table.

6. The principal feast of the Jewish calendar was the Passover which commemorated the Israelites' flight from Egyptian slavery and recalled their final meal in Egypt (Exodus C12).

7. The most famous of all miraculous feedings in the Old Testament was the manna provided in the desert (Exodus C16).

8. Other multiplications of food happened:

    a)   Elijah the prophet multiplied the oil in the widow's jug (1Kings 17:7-16),

    b)   Elisha the prophet multiplied the oil for the widow (2Kings 4:1-7) and the barley loaves for the one hundred men (2Kings 4:43-44).

9. These Old Testament stories prepared the stage for New Testament miracles and for the Eucharist.

NEW TESTAMENT
PREPARING FOR THE GIFT

Multiplication of Food

10.   In the gospels, the multiplication of loaves and fishes is reported six times, in all four gospels and twice in Matthew and Mark (Mt 14:13-21, Mt 15:32-38, Mk 6:34-44, Mk 8:1-9, Lk 9:12-17, Jn 6:1-15).

11. Obviously, this miracle was extremely important to the early Church, which saw this miracle as a preview of Jesus multiplying His own Real Presence in the Eucharist.

12. In John's gospel, this multiplication is immediately followed by Jesus' clearest and strongest remarks about the importance of receiving Holy Communion (6:25-59).

13. Jesus' most important teaching on Holy Communion is contained in John 6:52-58. In these few verses Jesus says:

a) Whoever does not eat and drink of the Eucharist has no life (V53)

b) Whoever does receive Holy Communion, Jesus will raise up on the last day (V54)

c) Whoever receives Holy Communion abides in Jesus (V56).

d) The recipient will have the same divine life that Jesus has from the Father (V57).

The Last Supper

14. All four gospels describe the Last Supper, a clear sign of its obvious importance.

15. Three gospels provide descriptions of Jesus' words at the Last Supper: (Mt 26:20-30; Mk 14:17-26; Lk 22:14-23).

16. The earliest New Testament teaching on the Last Supper comes from St. Paul (1Cor, C11) and contains these truths:

a) At the Last Supper, Jesus said over the bread, "This is my body which is for you, do this in remembrance of me."

b) Jesus said over the wine, "This cup is the new covenant in my blood. Do this whenever you drink it, in remembrance of me" (V 24-25).

c) By receiving Holy Communion, the believer proclaims the death of Jesus until He comes back (V 26).

d)   Because of these truths, going to Holy Communion unworthily is a sin against the Body and Blood of Christ (V 27).

17.   The three gospel accounts and Paul's description are based upon Christian liturgical practices that existed in Jerusalem, Antioch and Rome.

18.   Therefore, the tradition of Christian Eucharist obviously arose immediately after the Ascension of Jesus.

Meals With the Risen Jesus

19.   After Jesus rose from the dead, many vision accounts centered on eating a meal:
   a)   "Finally, as they were at table, Jesus was revealed to the eleven" (Mk 16:14).
   b)   The two disciples going to Emmaus didn't recognize Jesus until the Eucharist. "When He (Jesus) had seated himself with them to eat, He took bread, pronounced the blessing, then broke the bread, and began to distribute it to them. With that, their eyes were   opened   and   they   recognized   him" (Lk 24:30-31).
   c)   After Jesus showed the apostles His hands and feet, He asked, "Have you anything here to eat?" They gave him a piece of cooked fish which He took and ate in their presence (Lk 24:41-43).
   d)   When Jesus appeared to the apostles while they were fishing, He had a charcoal fire there with a fish laid in it and some bread.

"Bring some of the fish you just caught," Jesus told them (Jn 21:9).

20. Peter speaks clearly of Easter visions taking place at meals
" . . . but only by such witnesses as had been chosen beforehand by God - by us who ate and drank with him after he rose from the dead" (Acts 10:41).

21. This eating with Jesus after He rose from the dead teaches two things:
a) the reality of Jesus' Resurrection
b) the ever available gift of experiencing the Risen Jesus in the Eucharist.

Acts of the Apostles

22. After Pentecost, the early Church realized that the newly baptized believers should come together regularly for Eucharist. "They devoted themselves to the apostles' instruction and the communal life, to the breaking of the bread and the prayers" (Acts 2:43).

23. Paul celebrated Sunday Eucharist at Troas, "On the first day of the week, when we gathered for the breaking of the bread" (20:7).

EARLY CHURCH DOCUMENTS

Three church documents give extremely clear teaching on Christian Eucharistic faith and practice:
1. The Didache
2. The Jerusalem Catechism

The Eucharist

3. St. Justin's Defense of the Christians
(155 A.D.)

The Didache

24. The book called Didache (90 A.D.) records the actions of the bishop presiding at the Eucharistic gathering.

The Jerusalem Catechism

25. The Jerusalem Catechism has many clear statements about the Eucharist:

a) "Since Christ himself has declared the bread to be His body, who can have any further doubt?"

b) "Since He himself has said quite categorically, 'This is my blood', who would dare to question it and say that it is not His blood."

c) "Therefore, it is with complete assurance that we receive the bread and wine as the body and blood of Christ."

d) "Do not then regard the Eucharistic elements as ordinary bread and wine; they are in fact the body and blood of the Lord."

St. Justin's Defense of the Christians

Justin (Rome 155 A.D.)says the following:
Three conditions for receiving:
1) "No one can share the Eucharist with us unless he believes what we teach is true."

27. 2) "He must be washed in the regenerating
waters of baptism for the remission of sins."

3) "He must live in accordance with the
principles given us by Christ."

Day of Gathering

a) "On Sunday, we have a common assembly
of all our members"

b) "We hold our common assembly on Sunday
because it is the first day of the week, and because on
that same day our savior Jesus Christ rose from the
dead."

Explaining Christian Belief

a) "We do not consume the Eucharistic bread
as if it were ordinary food and drink."

b) The Eucharist "becomes the flesh and blood
of the incarnate Jesus by the power of his own words
contained in the Prayer of Thanksgiving."

Liturgy

a) Bread and wine and water are brought
forward. The president offers prayers and gives
thanks to the best of his ability.

b) The people give their ascent by saying
"Amen".

c) "The Eucharist is distributed; everyone
present communicates."

d) "The deacons take it to those who are
absent."

e) "The collection is placed in the custody of
the president who "takes care of all who are in need."

27. Hippolytus in his "The Apostolic Tradition" describes a full Eucharistic Rite and provides the basic content for the second Eucharistic prayer. This preserved document is the fullest and most important source of the Roman liturgy in the second and third century.

CATHOLIC BELIEF IN THE REAL PRESENCE

28. Many Christian churches, while celebrating Eucharist, do not believe in the Catholic doctrine of the Real Presence and do not see the Eucharist as of central importance.

29. This doctrine of the Real Presence was always believed by Catholics, because of the clear New Testament quotes, and the many early Christian documents.

COUNCIL OF TRENT

Even though Christianity was split in two (1054), both Churches, the Roman Catholic Church and the Eastern Orthodox maintained the full belief in the Eucharist which was passed down from the Apostolic Tradition. Only with the rise of Protestantism did the heresies about the Eucharist begin to seriously shake the Catholic Church. The Church gave its official response to these false Eucharistic teachings at the Council of Trent (1545-1563).

30. The Council responded to the false teachings of Luther, who believed in the Real Presence but only at the moment of receiving Holy Communion.

31. The Council also reacted against the more serious errors of the other Protestant leaders who denied any Real Presence and said that Christ was only dynamically present (Calvin) or only symbolically present (Zwingli).

32. These two Protestant teachers stressed that communion with Christ in the Eucharist is achieved only by the faith of the recipient; a total shift away from the true multiplication of Christ's Presence in our tabernacles.

33. The Council of Trent (1551) condemned all these errors as clearly as possible: "If anyone denies that the body and blood, together with the soul and divinity, of our Lord Jesus Christ, and therefore the whole Christ, is truly, really and substantially contained in the most holy Eucharist, but says that Christ is present in the Sacrament only as in a sign or a figure, or by His power, let him be anathema."

34. In a positive teaching the Council of Trent (1545-63) said: "After the consecration of the bread and wine, Our Lord Jesus Christ, true God and man, is truly, really and substantially contained under the perceptible species of bread and wine."

The Eucharist

35. For the past 450 years, Trent has set the Catholic Church on a clear road, totally committed to the Eucharist as the Real Presence of Jesus and the summit of worship of God.

Summary of Catholic Doctrine

36. The Real Presence of Christ within both the species, bread and wine, results from the Eucharistic Prayer said by the priest. This Presence continues as long as the bread and wine remain incorrupt.

37. Christ is present, whole and entire, in each species of bread and wine.

38. Catholics should receive Holy Communion whenever they attend Mass. Assisting at Mass on Sunday is a basic Catholic obligation.

Preparation for Receiving

39. Holy Communion can be received only by the baptized. (The holy water fonts at the Church entrances remind Catholics of their baptismal gift, allowing them to share at the Lord's table.)

40. The person must be fasting from food and drink (except water) for one hour. This rule does not apply to the sick.

41. The person must be in the state of grace, that is, not conscious of any serious sin committed since his or her last confession.

42. The person should be filled with faith in Jesus, with a loyalty to Jesus and a desire to spread His Kingdom.

43. Especially important is forgiveness and reconciliation. "If you bring your gift to the altar and then recall that your brother has anything against you, leave your gift at the altar, go first to be reconciled with your brother and then come and offer your gift" (Mt 5:23-24).

44. This reconciliation is symbolized by the Our Father and the Sign of Peace within the Mass.

The Fruits of Holy Communion

45. Obviously a personal union with the Risen Jesus by receiving Eucharist has effects beyond anyone's understanding. However, the following certainly should result from this gift

    a) increases our union with Jesus. "He who eats my flesh abides in me and I in him." (Jn.6:56)

    b) as material food has many effects upon human life, so this spiritual food affects our spiritual life of grace

    c) Christ's presence separates us from sin, cleanses of past sins and preserves us from future sins. (The Eucharist is not primarily ordered to forgiving serious sin, which is the role of the Sacrament of Reconciliation, but it certainly forgives any mortal sins of which the person is not aware. The Eucharist preserves from future serious sins.)

d)   The Eucharist unites to the Church, knitting those who receive more deeply into the Body of Christ.

e) " Because there is one bread, we who are many are one body, for we all partake of the one bread." (1Cor.10: 16-17)

f) The Eucharist commits the believers to help the poor.

g)   The Eucharist makes us aware of the division of the Churches, awakening us to bring about reconciliation.

GETTING TO HEAVEN

46.   The most important goal of the Eucharist is to get us to heaven.   Jesus likened the reign of God to a king who gave a wedding banquet for his son. (Mt.22:1-14) After many rejected the invitation, the king sent his servants to invite all.   This filled the wedding hall with banqueters. (V.10)

47. The best way of getting to God's heavenly banquet is to accept His weekly invitation to Jesus' earthly feast.

48.   Every time Eucharist is received, the believer's capacity to enjoy heaven is increased.   As Holy Communion increases our desire for heaven, sin is more easily rejected.

Eucharistic Adoration

49.   For the first eleven centuries, the Blessed Sacrament was reserved in the churches for the sick

but not kept for adoration. This changed in the twelfth and thirteenth centuries, which saw the growth of Eucharistic devotion culminating in the feast of Corpus Christi (1264).

50. In the twelfth and thirteenth centuries the faithful wanted to look at the host. Priests were told to raise the host at the consecration for the people to see and adore. A black cloth was hung behind the altar, so the people could easily see the white hosts. Also, the ringing of the bells announced this elevation.

51. Some priests made a second elevation before the Our Father. Others turned around so the people could see. Seeing the host became extremely important. Unfortunately, some Church councils prescribed that all heads be bowed. This was changed by Pope Pius X, who urged the faithful to look at the host.

Feast of Corpus Christi

52. A tremendous change happened in the thirteenth century with the establishing of the feast of Corpus Christi. This devotion began by a direct initiative of Jesus who appeared to St. Juliana, telling her that a feast honoring the Real Presence should be established.

53. St. Juliana saw a vision of a full moon, disfigured by a single dark spot.

54. Jesus explained that the feast of Holy Thursday focused on the Eucharist as sacrifice. He wanted

another feast devoted to the Eucharist as His Real Presence.

55. Juliana made this vision known to the bishop of Liege and in 1246, a diocesan feast of Corpus Christi was established at Liege.

56. She also told James Panteleon (Archdeacon of Liege) who was later elected Pope Urban IV (1261.)

57. In 1264, Pope Urban IV extended the feast of Corpus Christi to the whole world. Supposedly, the impetus for this proclamation came from a Eucharistic miracle (1263) in which blood seeped from a host consecrated by Father Peter of Prague at a Mass in Bolsena.

58. Due to this feast and the accompanying procession, the monstrance came into great popularity, allowing the people to see the host.

59. The people even wanted the monstrance to remain on the altar after Mass. The bishops, allowed the continual presence of the Eucharist at the altar but asked that the tabernacle be constructed for greater reverence.

Eucharistic Miracles

60. During the two thousand years that the Church has had this Real Presence of Jesus in the Eucharist, many Eucharistic miracles have happened.

61.These miracles include a great variety of manifestations. Such as the host bleeding; the host taking on the appearance of flesh; the wine taking on the appearance of blood and the hosts not decaying even though centuries pass.

62. One of these miracles of the host bleeding was actually filmed by a video camera (Betania, Venezuela, December 8, 1991). This host is now kept in the Bishop's Chapel.

63. These miracles are often needed to remove doubts about the Real Presence and to overcome the modern rationalism which denies supernatural intervention.

Conclusion

64. Going to Mass and receiving Holy Communion have always been the center of Catholic piety. This practice has solid basis in the New Testament and in Church tradition. Unfortunately, some Protestant reformers refused to believe that Jesus could be "really, truly, and substantially present" in the Eucharist. As a result, in other Christian churches, the Eucharist is often pushed aside to a lesser place than the central worship which it deserves.

CHAPTER 4

SACRAMENT OF RECONCILIATION

Definition

In the Sacrament of Reconciliation, the penitent, because truly sorry for his/her sins, confesses these sins to a priest, who, in the name of Jesus and in the power of the Church forgives those sins by the prayer of absolution. Any sins forgotten by the penitent are also forgiven. In reparation, the penitent accepts whatever penance the priest imposes.

Three Names

Reconciliation

1.   Reconciliation is the sacrament's newest name, stressing the removal of any walls between God and the person and between believers. "We implore you, in Christ's name: be reconciled to God." (2Cor 5:20)

2.   The name also stresses the oneness demanded among believers: "Leave your gift at the altar, go first to be reconciled with your brother and then come and offer your gift." (Mt5:24)

3.   God's ministry of reconciliation is now given to the Church. "All this has been done by God, who has reconciled us to himself through Christ and has given us the ministry of reconciliation." (2Cor 5:18)

Penance

4. Penance was the official name of the sacrament before Vatican Council II. This name stresses the internal spirit of the person, called the penitent, who should approach this sacrament with inner sorrow and a willingness to change. This name also applies to the prayers or spiritual task assigned by the priest after the confessing of sins.

Confession

5. Confession is the popular name for this sacrament, stressing the difficult duty of the penitents to examine their conscience and to declare their sins to the priest.

SCRIPTURAL BACKGROUND

OLD TESTAMENT

6. The forgiveness of sins was an important gift which God gave to the Israelites, as is clear from the following examples.

7. In the Old Testament, God established:
    a) sin offerings according to a person's state in life (Lev. C4) and also special sacrifices for individual sins (Lev. C5)
    b) an annual special Day of Atonement (Yom Kippur) "Once a year atonement shall be made for all the sins of the Israelites." (Lev. 16:34)

c)   a sin offering (one he-goat) for inadvertent sins of the people (Num.15:22-24).

8.   Sins were also forgiven through the intercession of Moses (Ex 32:30-34)

9.   Isaiah stresses God's gift of pardon: "I have brushed away your offenses like a cloud, your sins like a mist." (Is.44:22) and prophesies that the Suffering Servant will "take away the sins of many and win pardon for their offenses." (Is. 53:12)

10. God's willingness to forgive reaches its height in the promise of an entirely New Covenant, "for I will forgive their evildoing and remember their sins no more". (Jer.31: 31-34)

NEW TESTAMENT

Jesus' Ministry

11.   The gospels record four specific people who directly received forgiveness from Jesus:

a) the paralyzed man: "Have courage, son, your sins are forgiven."(Mt.9:6) (cf Mk2:5, Lk5:20)

b)   the penitent woman who washed His feet: "He then said to her, 'Your sins are forgiven'". (Lk.7:48)

c)   the adulterous woman: "Nor do I condemn you. You may go. But from now on avoid this sin." (Jn.8:11).

d) the Good Thief: "I assure you, this day you will be with me in paradise." (Lk23:43)

12. Jesus foresaw His death as an opportunity for all to receive forgiveness: "The Son of Man has come 'to give his own life as a ransom for the many'" (Mt.20:28)13. At the Last Supper, Jesus repeated this promise:

"This is my blood, the blood of the New Covenant, to be poured out in behalf of many for the forgiveness of sins." (Mt.26:28)

Jesus Giving Power to His Church

13. Jesus promised Peter the keys of the kingdom and the power to bind or to loose. "I will entrust to you the keys of the kingdom of heaven. Whatever you declare bound on earth, shall be bound in heaven; whatever you declare loosed on earth, shall be loosed in heaven." (Mt16:19)

14. He later promised the same powers to the twelve apostles. (Mt.18:18)

15. On Easter Sunday night, Jesus gave this power to his disciples who were in the Upper Room: "Receive the Holy Spirit. If you forgive men's sins, they are forgiven them; if you hold them bound, they are held bound." (Jn.20: 22-23)

THE APOSTLES UNDERSTANDING

16.   Many New Testament texts speak of receiving forgiveness of sins through Jesus but some of these obviously refer to Baptism. For example, in the Acts of the Apostles, the basic preaching to accept Jesus as Savior stressed the forgiveness of sins through Baptism.

17.   Some New Testament texts, however, speak clearly of the Church's power to forgive sins committed after Baptism.

     a) James is clearly speaking to already baptized Christians when he writes: "Hence, declare your sins to one another and pray for one another, that you might find healing." (5:16)

     b) Paul speaks of himself and the Corinthian community reconciling a sinner. (2Cor 2:5-11)

     c) John writes to the Church of Ephesus: "Keep firmly in mind the heights from which you have fallen. Repent and return to your former deeds." (Rev.2:5)

     d) And to the Church of Pergamum: "Therefore, repent! If you do not, I will come to you soon and fight against them with the sword of my mouth." (2:16)

18.   Therefore, many New Testament texts speak of repentance, forgiveness and reconciliation for believers after Baptism. This is the focus of the Sacrament of Reconciliation, the forgiveness of sins after sacramental Baptism.

EARLY CHURCH WRITERS

19. An early second century writer (the Shepherd of Hermas) describes a second penance after Baptism that was entrusted by Jesus to the Shepherd (i.e. the bishop).

20. Other early writers exhort all believers to repentance for forgiveness of sins (Clement, Ignatius, and Polycarp).

21. Early heresies denied the Bishop's power to forgive sins, but Tertullian ("On Penance") holds out hope for all sinners and urges them to use the liturgical penance of the Church.

EARLY CHURCH HISTORY

22. Over the centuries, the exact form in which the Church has forgiven sins has varied greatly.

23. Because the early Church existed primarily in cities, the liturgical forgiving of sins was administered directly by the bishop.

24. The early Church stressed forgiveness for three grave sins: adultery, murder and sacrificing to idols to avoid persecution.

Reconciliation

25. This forgiveness was sought publicly and given publicly after the performance of public penance (sometimes only after years of penance).

26. Penitents approached the bishop on Ash Wednesday, performed their public penance during Lent and were reconciled on Holy Thursday.

28. As the Church expanded into rural areas, some functions, such as forgiving sins, were exercised also by priests.

28. In the seventh century, the Irish monks came to Europe to rekindle the faith. Their apostolic ministry focused on private confession (as we have it today). Frequently, the priest missionary carried a portable confessional with him.

29. Since the seventh century, private individual confession administered by a priest has replaced public confession and public penance assigned by the bishop.

30. This confessional form exists today and includes the gifts of frequent confession and forgiveness of venial and mortal sins in one sacramental celebration.

31. Throughout history, two essential elements are the same:
     a) The personal inner conversion shown by sorrow, confessing of sins and acceptance of penance

b) God's forgiving action through the Church's priests

32. Every priest who hears confessions is bound by a strict Church rule (C 1388) called the "sacramental seal of confession". By this seal, the priest must maintain absolute secrecy concerning the sins told to him in confession.

NEED FOR THIS SACRAMENT

33. The three sacraments of initiation (Baptism, Confirmation and Eucharist) establish the believer in a state of holiness. However, they do not abolish all human weakness nor destroy the power of sin (called concupiscence) within the believer. Although gifted by the initiation sacraments with a holiness which requires the exclusion of sin, the baptized realizes that "If we say we have no sin, we deceive ourselves . . ." (1Jn1:8)

34. The baptized actually undertakes a life committed to an uninterrupted task of constant conversion.

35. Daily experience shows that this task is not one continual victory, but is always marred by some lapses, sometimes of a serious nature.

36. By the Sacrament of Reconciliation, the Church is present when the Christian, under the power of inner grace, wants to take up anew this task of constant conversion.

VALUE OF CONFESSING SINS TO A PRIEST

37.   Modern psychiatry focuses on the value of describing inner conflicts and sins.

38.   Sacramental confession adds a spiritual dimension to this process namely, the power of Jesus given to the Church to actually forgive these sins and bring about healing on all levels.

39.   A frequent use of confession:

a)   develops a spiritual honesty within the penitent

b)   removes much inner conflict over guilt feelings

c)   provides a forum for receiving spiritual advice

d)   focuses the person on those aspects of life which need special vigilance

e)   frees from the powers of addiction

f)   empowers the person for true holiness

40.   Priests are trained to be merciful in this sacrament, to be honest but never harsh with the penitent.   Priests and penitents must see this sacrament as an instrument of God's mercy.

Duties of the Penitent

41.   The duties of the penitent are clear:

a)   an honest examination of conscience to recall what sins have been committed.

b) telling these sins to a priest

c) a sincere desire to turn away from these sins (even though a frail human nature might commit them again).

d) some satisfaction to God by fulfilling the penance imposed by the priest.

DIFFICULTIES WITH CONFESSION

42. Many Catholics experience special problems with this sacrament, which frequently leads to the question, "Why must I tell my sins to the priest?"

43. The root cause of this question usually lies in some personal difficulty the Catholic is experiencing or has experienced.

44. The more common difficulties (with some answers) are the following:

a) In previous confessions, the Catholic has not been able to speak or to explain all his/her sins. Thus, the past darkness has not been cleared up.

Answer:

Mention in a general way the inability in the past to confess everything. Most priests will not want to delve into past memories.

b) There is a natural sense of shame and guilt concerning personal sins. Even in human relationships, admitting to sinful behavior is difficult.

Answer:

Think of the joy that comes by getting the sins forgiven and getting beyond the guilt feelings.

c) The Catholic has gone to confession in the past, told their sins, and then committed these same sins again, leading to discouragement.

Answer:

Continue to use the sacrament. At times, there are addictions, which are not removed immediately. Confession often prevents the spread of the problem and depression over past sins.

d) The Catholic is involved with serious sin that he/she does not want to give up.

Answer:

Just honestly submit all this to the priest confessor. Confession itself is a first step not a final conclusion.

OBJECTIONS TO THE SACRAMENT

45. Catholics wonder why they need to confess their sins to receive forgiveness, while other Christian churches do not teach this need.

Answer:

1) Sacramental confession was a teaching of the Church until Luther revolted in the 16th Century. The Greek Orthodox Church has this Sacrament of Reconciliation just as the Roman Catholic Church.

The rejection of this sacrament began with Protestantism.

2) Without this sacrament, the Protestant Churches do not provide for their members the power and the consolation of sacramental forgiveness. In other words, some special gifts of Jesus were lost in the 16th Century Protestant denial of some Catholic sacraments.

46. Protestants claim that this sacrament is an excuse, allowing Catholics to continue to commit sin.

Answer:

1) God's forgiveness and God's mercy can be misused. Obviously, some Catholics approach this sacrament with far from perfect motives. However, most Catholics approach the sacrament in great sincerity and find, in this sacrament, a constant help to keep the commandments, not a false freedom to continue sinning.

2) In Catholic history, many heresies claimed that any Church practice of reconciling sinners was too lax. Popes had to state the Catholic teaching that God's mercy is always available to the repentant sinner. Some people are always scandalized by the Church reconciling sinners to God. Even when Jesus forgave sins, many were scandalized.

CONCLUSION

47. Reconciliation is an extremely important sacrament because people are easily confused about moral issues. People tend to believe that nothing is

wrong with what they are doing. Even Catholics who have a correct sense of morality often wander from the straight and narrow.

48. The confessional is a place of honesty and mercy. The priest pronounces the sentence, "guilty, but pardoned in Jesus' name." In many ways, the confessional is the most consoling place on earth. A Catholic can be assured of receiving God's forgiveness while hearing the words, "Go and sin no more."

49. A priest friend deeply devoted to his ministry in this sacrament had a favorite saying, "For most of us the door to heaven is the door of the confessional."

CHAPTER 5

THE ANOINTING OF THE SICK

Definition

The Anointing of the Sick is the sacrament by which a baptized person receives forgiveness of their sins, healing of mind, body and soul, and needed strength to face death, when that ensues.

The Problem of Illness and Death

1. Illness and death present the gravest of human problems, often leading to great anguish and sometimes to despair and revolt against God.

2. Jesus, in the gospels, spends much time with the sick. His power over sin, illness and death show that "God has visited His people." (Lk.7:16)

3. Often Jesus used signs to heal (spittle, laying on of hands, mud and washing). These signs prefigure this sacrament of anointing.

Jesus' Victory

4. Paul wrote clearly that death entered the world through sin "... through one man sin entered the world and with sin death, death thus coming to all men". (Rom 5:12.

5. Paul also claims a greater victory in Jesus, "much more did the grace of God, and the gracious gift of the one man, Jesus Christ, abound for all." (Rom.5:15)

Anointing of the Sick

6. Jesus, however, overcame sin and death. Paul calls this "the gracious gift of the one man, Jesus Christ," which is meant to "abound for all".
(Rom 5:15)

Old Testament

7. Some preview of Jesus' healing ministry exists in the Old Testament.

8. Moses healed those people who were bitten by the seraph serpents by placing a seraph on a pole, "whenever anyone who had been bitten by a serpent looked at the bronze serpent, he recovered" (Num 21:9).

9. Hezekiah was healed by Isaiah the prophet and fifteen years were added to his life (Is 38:1-8).

10. Naaman, the leper, was healed as he washed in the Jordan River at the Command of Elisha, the prophet. (2Kg:5)

11. Both Elijah (1Kg:17:17-24) and Elisha (2Kg.4:31-37) raised someone from the dead.

12. Isaiah prophesies Jerusalem as a place of healing, "No one who dwells there will say, 'I am sick'" (Is 33:24).

13. As God led the Israelites out of Egypt, He declared, "I, the Lord, am your healer" (Ex 15:26).

14. Although healing exists in the Old Testament, these healing stories are not as frequent or as powerful as those in the gospels.

The New Testament

Jesus' Extraordinary Powers

15. Jesus manifests an extraordinary power of healing, which led the crowds to bring all their sick to Him. "After sunset, as evening drew on, they brought to him all who were ill and those possessed by demons" (Mk 1:32).

16. The results of Jesus' power are astounding: "As a consequence of this, his reputation traveled the length of Syria. They carried to him all those afflicted with various diseases and racked with pain, the possessed, the lunatics, and the paralyzed. He cured them all" (Mt 4:24).

17. On three occasions Jesus raised the dead to life:
    a) The daughter of Jairus: "Taking her hand he said to her, 'Talitha, koum!'" which means, Little girl, get up(Mk 5:41). See also Luke 8:40-56.
    b) The son of the widow of Naim: "Jesus said, 'Young man, I bid you get up.' The dead man sat up and began to speak" (Lk 7:11-17).
    c) Lazarus, the brother of Martha and Mary: "Jesus called out loudly, 'Lazarus, come out!' The dead man came out, bound hand and foot with linen strips, his face wrapped in a cloth" (Jn 11:43-44).

Anointing of the Sick

Jesus Bestowing These Powers on the Church

18. Jesus promised that His healing ministry would continue: "Signs like these will accompany those who have professed their faith: they will use my name to expel demons; ...and the sick upon whom they lay their hands will recover" (Mk 16:17-18).

19. In fact, Jesus promised even greater powers: "I solemnly assure you, the man who has faith in me will do the works I do, and greater far than these" (Jn 14:12).

20. Jesus has fulfilled this promise. In two thousand years, millions have been healed in His name

21. Especially in our day, the miracle working power of the Holy Spirit is manifested in great signs and wonders.

The Ministry of the Apostles

22. After Jesus ascended into heaven, the apostles continued His healing ministry.

23. The Acts of the Apostles records Peter:
   a) healing a lame man (3:1-9)
   b) healing all upon whom his shadow fell. "The people carried the sick into the streets and laid them on cots and mattresses, so that when Peter passed by at least his shadow might fall on one or another of them.
   Crowds from the towns around Jerusalem would gather, too, bringing their sick and those who were

troubled by unclean spirits, all of whom were cured" (5:15-16)
    c) healing the paralytic at Aeneas (9:32-35)
    d) raising Tabitha from the dead (9:36-43)

24. Philip performed miracles in Samaria, "Many others were paralytics or cripples, and these were cured" (14:8-10).

25. The Acts record Paul with similar powers:
    a) healing a lame man (14:8-10)
    b) healing all by handkerchiefs: "Meanwhile God worked extraordinary miracles at the hands of Paul. When handkerchiefs or cloths which had touched his skin were applied to the sick, their diseases were cured and evil spirits departed from them" (19:11-12)
    c) healing a lame man at Lystra (14:8-13)
    d) raising the dead boy, Eutychus, to life (20:7-12)

The Letter of James

26. The Council of Trent (1551) stated clearly that "this sacred anointing of the sick ...is alluded to by Mark but is recommended to the faithful and promulgated by James ..."

27. Trent is referring to the Letter of James, "Is there anyone sick among you? He should ask for the presbyters of the Church. They, in turn, are to pray over him, anointing him with oil in the name of the Lord. This prayer uttered in faith will reclaim the one

who is ill, and the Lord will restore him to health. If he has committed any sins, forgiveness will be his. Hence, declare your sins to one another and pray for one another, that you may find healing" (5:14-16). Obviously, this is an extremely important text!

28.   The Council of Trent noted that Mark's gospel prefigured this text of James, when Mark wrote of anointing with oil: "They (the twelve) expelled many demons, anointed the sick with oil, and worked many cures " (6:13).

29. By his clear words, James foresees a restoration of bodily health resulting from this ritual prayer.

30. James also includes forgiveness of grave sins as a power of this sacrament.

31.   James describes a very ill Christian and the local leaders of the Church (presbyters). He is not speaking of the charism of healing but implies an extension of the power of Baptism. ("In the name of the Lord" was the way believers were baptized in the Acts.)

32.   For believers, the moment of grave illness is a special time to reaffirm their baptismal commitment.

History of the Church

33. Early writings make some references to this anointing. In the early fifth century, Pope Innocent I defined that:
    a) the letter of James refers to this sacrament

b)　the oil must be blessed by the bishop

c)　both bishops and priests can anoint

d)　this anointing completes the Sacrament of Penance.

34.　St. Augustine (5th century) "was accustomed to visiting the sick who desired it in order to lay his hands on them and pray at their bedsides." He also incorporated James' admonition.

35. Hippolytus in his "Apostolic Traditions" (the clearest and most detailed explanation of the late second century Roman liturgy) has a formula for the blessing of the oil for the sick.

Effects

36. The Council of Trent clearly explained the sacrament's effects:

a)　the removal of sins if any still need to be expiated

b)　comfort and strength

c)　bestowal of hope in God's mercy

d)　strength to accept the trials of illness

e)　power to overcome the temptations of the devil

f)　occasionally, restoring health to the body if this would be for the advantage of the soul.

37.　Although this sacrament is usually received by a person in grace, it might be received by a person who cannot confess their sins. In this case, the sacrament forgives sins, as a direct effect.

Bodily Well-Being

38. Although Trent speaks of occasional restoration to health, this sacrament has bodily well-being as an essential effect because:

    a) Bodily health and spiritual grace are interlocked in this sacrament, which sees a oneness of the person's body and soul.

    b) Bodily infirmity can often hinder a person's oneness with God. It is a disorder brought about by sin.

    c) Often, the sick person, so consumed by the illness, cannot focus on God.

39. The sacrament, even when not fully restoring to health, should always remove those aspects of the illness which are potentially destructive of grace.

40. Sometimes the sacrament's power results in an inner harmony, in a sudden cure or, at least, a more rapid recovery.

Preparing For Death

41. If the sickness leads to death, the person receives the following:

    a) strength against the final temptations of the evil one

    b) faith to be united with Jesus' sufferings and even consecrated to enter more deeply into Jesus' passion

42. The sacraments of Penance and Eucharist (as Viaticum, food for the journey) should also be received.

43. As three sacraments (Baptism, Confirmation and Eucharist) constitute Christian Initiation, so three sacraments (Penance, Anointing of the Sick and Eucharist) constitute the final sacramental gifts of the Church to the dying believer.

CHAPTER 6

MATRIMONY

Definition

Matrimony is the sacrament in which a baptized man and woman, by their mutual consent, enter into a spiritual relationship and receive all the needed graces to preserve their lifelong commitment to each other.

Marriage and Matrimony

1. In the Church's terminology, marriage is a natural contract. Matrimony is this same natural contract raised to the dignity of a Church sacrament.

2. A valid marriage between a baptized man and woman is also the sacrament of matrimony.

3. Based mainly upon Paul's teaching in 1Cor C7, the Church has defined Christian matrimony as:
   a. a covenant (sacred commitment)
   b. between a man and a woman
   c. to share their life together
   d. to accept sexual relations which are open to the procreation of children
   e. this covenant is permanent (lasting until the death of the partner)
   f. and requires fidelity (the spouse cannot have sexual relations with anyone else).

4. The Catholic Church teaches that Jesus restored marriage to its original dignity and also conferred upon

the baptized unique graces to help them to live as "married in the Lord."

Book of Genesis

5. Marriage occupies the very opening chapters of the Bible (Book of Genesis).

<u>God's Plan</u>

6. Man is made in the image and likeness of God (Gen 1:26 and 27)

7. God made mankind male and female (1:27)

8. Procreation flows from God's special blessing (1:28)

9. After naming all the animals, Adam found that "none proved to be a suitable partner" (2:20)

10. To solve this problem, God created woman directly (2:22). The symbol of Adam's rib shows that woman is to be at man's side (2:21).

11. Their marital relationship is so important that it breaks other relational bonds. "That is why a man leaves his father and mother". (2:23).

12. This marital relationship is meant to be the deepest and most intimate. Adam exclaims, "This one, at last, is bone of my bones and flesh of my flesh" (2:23).

The Breakdown of God's Ideal Relationship

13. The first book of the Bible also records the sin of Adam and Eve causing the breakdown of the relationship and the destruction of the initial intimacy:

a) Adam and Eve feel shame because they are naked (Gen 3:10-11).

b) They disagree on the causes of their new problems **(3:12-13).**

God's Help

14. To counteract these problems caused by sin, God begins immediately to help the couple. "For the man and his wife, the Lord God made leather garments with which he clothed them" (En 3:32).

15. God also moves to protect mankind from inflicting unchangeable damage upon the human family. God stationed "the cherubim and the fiery resolving sword to guard the way to the tree of life." (Gen.3:24)

Genesis Teaching

16. This quick overview of Genesis reveals a clear teaching on marriage:

a) God's focus in creation is the formation of parents who would live in intimacy and multiply.

b) To foster this, God bestowed special gifts upon Adam and Eve.

c) Although some of these gifts were lost, God still intended parents to stay together, and to fulfill His original plan of procreation.

Old Testament Practice

20. This ideal of marriage given in Genesis was rarely attained among the Israelites, although the prophets claimed that God's love for His people was totally faithful.

21. The increased power of sin eroded this marriage ideal. Divorce, and even polygamy, are tolerated in the Old Testament.

22. The Old Testament, however, begins to point to the ideal of marriage in the beautiful stories of Ruth and Tobias, as well as the prophets' picturing of God as a faithful husband to His people, Israel.

Gospels

23. Jesus states clearly that He planned to restore marriage as it was before the fall of Adam. (The Kingdom of God inaugurated by Jesus has power to turn back the effects of sin.)

24. Jesus' goal is the original creation plan of His Father: "At the beginning of creation God made them male and female; for this reason a man shall leave his father and mother and the two shall become as one. They are no longer two but one flesh" (Mk 10: 6-8).

25. Jesus saw Moses' granting divorce as a compromise due to the stubbornness of the Israelites (Mk 10:5).

26. Jesus revokes Moses' power to grant divorce: "Therefore let no man separate what God has joined" (Mk 10:9).

27. Jesus blessed the holiness of marriage by attending the wedding feast of Cana (Jn C2).

Paul's Teaching on Christian Marriage

27. In his first letter to the Corinthians, St. Paul gives extensive teaching on Christian marriage:

   a) The married should stay together: "A wife must not separate from her husband."

   b) If separated, the spouse cannot remarry: "If she does separate she must either remain single or become reconciled to him again." Similarly, a husband must not divorce his wife (1Cor. 7:11).

   c) The couple should stay together even if the partner is not a believer in Jesus. "If any brother has a wife who is an unbeliever but is willing to live with him, he must not divorce her" (1Cor 7:12).

30. The married couple should not withhold sexual activity from the other: "The husband should fulfill his conjugal obligations toward his wife, the wife towards her husband" (1Cor 7:3).

31. Marriage is a legitimate choice for a believer: "To avoid immorality, every man should have his own wife and every woman her own husband" (1Cor 7:2).

32 Marriage is an honorable vocation: "The man who marries his virgin acts fittingly" (1Cor 7:38). "Let marriage be honored in every way" (Heb 13:4).

33. Marriage creates a life-long bond: "A wife is bound to her husband as long as he lives" (1Cor 7:39). "A married woman is bound to her husband by law while he lives" (Rom 7:2).

34. Death of one's spouse frees the other to marry again: "If her husband dies, she is free to marry again, but on one condition, that it be in the Lord" (1Cor 7:39).

MARRIAGE IN THE LORD

Paul's Thinking

35. Paul saw Baptism making the believer a new creation, which deeply and radically affected their lives.

36. The union of two believers in marriage was a unique gift, called by Paul "marriage in the Lord." (7:39)

37. This marriage between two baptized believers was different because if one departed the other could not remarry (7:11).

38 Even if the spouse dies, Paul allows remarriage "on one condition, that it be in the Lord" (7:39).

MARRIAGE IN OUR DAY

39. Living a Christian marriage has never been easy. However, the Christian culture supported couples in their efforts. Today, marriage is under severe attack, both in theory and through the extraordinary pressures that militate against permanency, fidelity and the raising of children.

Making a Choice

40. For most Catholics, the most important decision in their life will be the choice of their marriage partner.

41. This selecting process takes time and is filled with much pain and often, poor choices (see my pamphlet "How to Marry the Right Person").

42. Certain basic rules will help in the selection process:
    a) try to marry within your own culture
    b) marry someone of your own faith (common religious practice is the greatest power in binding a couple together)
    c) Expect the person to keep the ten commandments
    d) Look carefully at the home background (called the family of origin)
    e) Break off a relationship that involves:
       - physical abuse
       - severe verbal abuse

      - alcohol abuse or drug abuse

      - promiscuity

      - lying and failure to keep basic commitments

    f)   Get advice. Talk to those who love you. Listen to your parents. Ask your siblings what they think. In other words, don't make the decision totally on your own.

    g)   Above all, get your own life in order. Practice your religious faith. Attend Church. Keep the Commandments. In this way, your choice will not be the result of a confused life style.

    h) Do not have sexual relations before marriage. (This is an important, but frequently seen as an out-dated piece of advice.) Pre-marital abstinence shows that the two people care about God's ways, have a respect for each other and have the personal strength to postpone immediate selfish gratification.

When Married

44. Advice on marriage fills volumes. The only advice suitable for this booklet is the following:

45. Your Catholic tradition has a wealth of teaching about life, especially the Ten Commandments, the duty of weekly mass attendance, and a Catholic life style. This Catholic tradition contains much wisdom. Accept it and you will be blessed. Reject it and you will reap the wrong harvest.

Matrimony

Pre-Marital Sex

46. Today, birth control devices are freely distributed in public schools which gives the wrong message - "Have sex but make it safe sex."

47. Modern television and movies presuppose that young people have sexual intercourse very early on, even in the most casual of relationships.

48.. This cultural brainwashing fosters superficial relationships. The partners, while having sexual relations, have never sorted out their emotions and are blinded to the real issues they should be honestly facing.

49. Jesus taught just the opposite, asking a man not even to look with lust upon a woman (Mt 5:28).

50. Pre-marital abstinence is no foolproof means of choosing the right marriage partner, but it certainly helps avoid choosing the wrong partner (and saves a lot of devastating emotions).

PROBLEMS WITHIN MARRIAGE

Infidelity

51. Infidelity, like pre-marital sex, is seen as a normal, to be expected, part of American life.

52. However, human nature hasn't changed and infidelity introduces extremely difficult obstacles to marital happiness.

53. Experts agree, infidelity causes everyone to suffer - the person, the spouse and the children.

54. Don't be fooled into thinking that fidelity is no longer an important aspect of marriage. You might find yourself without a spouse or family because you bought into the world's thinking.

Pornography

55. Pornography is now a universal problem, available everywhere. The following needs to be said:

a) Pornography is an addiction that can entrap anyone.

b) Once allowed to enter, pornography tends to quickly spread and is difficult to overcome.

c) As the pornographic addiction grows within the person, the spouse ceases to be the only source of sexual gratification, and the marriage suffers.

d) When pornography becomes the only, or the main source of sexual gratification, the marriage is in serious trouble and the couple should seek counseling or a return to the sacraments for help.

Abortion

56. Americans are fed the big lie that abortions in a medical facility are safe. No matter how well the

abortion is done, it cannot save the mother from the terrible feelings that will flow for the rest of her lifetime.

57. Abortion can kill marital love and deeply affect the ability of parents to offer a guilt-free love to their living children.

58. The most damaging effect comes when a wife has an abortion because her husband threatens to leave. Often, he leaves anyway. She ends up with no husband and no child.

58. It is important that couples agree before they marry that there will never be an abortion at any time or in any circumstances. If this commitment cannot be given before marriage, then the couple should not marry.

Artificial Contraception

59. No teaching of the Catholic Church is so controversial, so contradicted even by other Christian denominations or so unaccepted by its own members as its teaching against the use of artificial contraceptives in marriage.

60. This happened because other Christian Churches changed their moral teaching (Before 1930, every Christian Church condemned contraception). Because of this change, society now faces other serious moral questions: abortion, premarital and extra-marital sexuality and homosexuality.

61. A society imbued with a contraceptive-mentality inevitably becomes a sexually permissive society, because rejecting the union of sexual pleasure with the duty of procreation leads logically to many other selfish sexual decisions.

62. The Church teaches that God has built into the woman's body a cycle of fertility and infertility. This cycle is God's plan for couples to choose to conceive or not to conceive.

63. Unfortunately, this natural approach to implement a couple's decision is set aside, as of little value.

64. In its place, our culture places birth control pills, with many side effects, or mechanical means, which allow the couple to have intercourse whenever they wish. There is little need for the couple to communicate or to abstain out of concern for the other party or for the good of the family.

Other Evils

65. The contraceptive mentality also leads to abortion, which is seen as a legitimate means of birth control if contraceptive pills or devices fail.

66. Contraception encourages pre-marital sexual activity, since the normal deterrent of a possible pregnancy is removed.

67. Contraception totally changes lifestyles. Armed with contraceptives, young couples feel quite free to

live together, to vacation together (like a honeymoon couple) and to assume all the privileges of the married, while refusing to accept the duties of married life, because they have removed the procreative aspect of sexual relations.

Divorce

68. In Jesus' time, a great debate took place among Jewish rabbis concerning the reasons needed by a husband to divorce his wife (Mt 19:3-7; Mk 10:2-12).

69. When Jesus was confronted with the divorce question, he focused instead on the story in Genesis and how God had made marriage in the beginning as a permanent relationship (Mt 19:4-6; Mk 10:6-9; also Lk 16:18).

70. Later, when the apostles claimed that Jesus' teaching on the permanence of this commitment was impossible to keep, Jesus spoke of the commitment to God's kingdom (Mt 19:10-12; Mk 11:29-30). In other words, because the Holy Spirit comes in all the sacraments, Christian husbands and wives could keep the marriage covenant until death.

71. From the above, we can see that Jesus planned to do two things:
    a) reestablish the marriage ideal described in the first two chapters of the Bible.
    b) bestow the power to live up to that ideal by sending His Holy Spirit upon believers.

72. In the first half of the 20th century, the power of the Spirit established a powerful Christian culture in which divorce was rare. Unfortunately, evil powers have destroyed that culture

73. Because reshaping the culture seems impossible, the individual couple, to avoid divorce, must personally immerse themselves in weekly worship and daily family prayer. They must also turn off the television and make a radical commitment to go against the culture. Every other marriage will be swept away by our American culture.

CHAPTER 7

HOLY ORDERS - THE WORDS

<u>Definition</u>

Holy Orders is a sacrament whereby a bishop, by the laying on of hands and the appropriate prayers, ordains a baptized man to the order of deacon, priest or bishop.

Explaining the Vocabulary

1. The Church borrowed the word <u>Orders</u> from Roman usage where it meant a social body distinct from the people (such as the Roman Senate).

2. The Church used <u>Orders</u> to describe the clergy as set apart from the people.

3. Later, the same word was used to distinguish among the clergy in three different orders - of bishops, of priests and of deacons.

4. The Church also borrowed the Roman word <u>ordination</u> meaning the appointing of a person to a definite order.

<u>SCRIPTURAL BASIS</u>

OLD TESTAMENT

5. From the earliest periods, Levites performed priestly services in Israel. Their faithfulness to Moses resulted in his official rewarding of them, "Today you have been dedicated to the Lord" (EX 32:29).

6.   Eventually, worship became centralized in Jerusalem and, at the time of Jesus, priests were divided into twenty-four groups that took weekly turns in the temple (cf LK 1:5-9).

7.   At one point, the priestly role in Israel included guarding the temple, offering sacrifice, delivering oracles and instructing people in the traditions of Israel.

8.   Eventually, the priestly role was limited to offering sacrifice.

9.   This offering of priestly sacrifice in Israel ceased after 70 AD, when the Jerusalem temple was destroyed by the Romans.

NEW TESTAMENT

Authority and Sacraments

Because Holy Orders in the Catholic Church involves two different aspects, authority and sacramental powers, we will treat each separately.

Jesus Bestowing Authority

10.   All four gospels give a clear picture that Jesus chose twelve very special men as his apostles (MT 10:2; MK 3:16; LK 6:13; JN 6:67).

10.   Peter was the clear leader of the twelve and Jesus gave him the keys of the kingdom of heaven and

promised to build His Church upon him. "I for my part declare to you, you are 'Rock" and on this rock I will build my church and the jaws of death shall not prevail against it. I will entrust to you the keys of the kingdom of heaven" (MT 16:18).

12. Luke carefully notes that, after Jesus ascended into heaven, the eleven remaining apostles returned to Jerusalem (Acts 1:13) where Peter initiated an election that resulted in Matthias being named to the place of Judas (Acts 1:15-16).

13. This election shows the great importance of the twelve apostles, the foundation of Jesus' Church.

14. Even the heavenly Jerusalem will have the twelve apostles as its foundation. "The wall of the city had twelve courses of stones as its foundation, on which were written the names of the twelve apostles of the Lamb" (Rev 21:14).

15. The Church sees in Peter and the other eleven apostles the scriptural basis for the papacy and the worldwide episcopacy.

16. Because Jesus appeared to him on the road to Damascus, Paul also enjoyed apostolic authority. "Last of all, he was seen by me, as one born out of the normal course. I am the least of the apostles" (1Cor 15:8-9).

17. Paul writes clearly, "God has set up in the Church, first apostles ..." (1Cor 4:9).

The Church Passing On Authority

18. As the decades went by, and the original apostles died out, the need to continue this apostolic office for the sake of the Church became clear.

19. Paul laid hands upon Timothy, consecrating him to the office of bishop. "For this reason I remind you to stir into flames the gift of God that you have through the imposition of hands" (2Tim 1:6).

20. Paul gave Titus the mandate to do the same. "For this reason I left you in Crete, that you might .appoint presbyters in every town, as I directed you" (Titus 1:5).

21. This office of bishop is so important that Paul gives lengthy instructions on the qualifications of a bishop (1Tim 1:1-7), on his expectations of Timothy (1Tim 4:6-5:24) and on the duties of an apostle (2Tim 1-5).

22. Paul instructs Titus on the qualities needed for ordination (Titus 1:5-9) and Titus' own responsibilities as a bishop (Titus 2:1-8). He also gives him advice for the office (3:8-11).

23. These texts made evident that, by the end of the New Testament, the rite of laying on of hands was a clear method of passing on the apostolic authority bestowed by Jesus.

Holy Orders

24.   Besides bishops, Paul's writings attest to two other offices – "the appointment of presbyters (Priests)" (Titus 1:5) and the office of deacon (Phil 1:1 and 1 Tim 3: 8-13)

25.   The letters of St. Ignatius of Antioch (107 A.D.) show that many local churches already had a three-fold structure of orders - bishop, priest and deacon.

Sacramental Powers

26. Besides teaching and governing authority within the Church, bishops, priests and deacons are the ordinary ministers of sacraments.

27.   Bishops and priests have certain important sacramental powers in common (i.e., both are equally able) which are not shared in any way by others. These include:
    a) celebrating Mass
    b) forgiving sins in the Sacrament of
Reconciliation
    c) administering the Sacrament of the Anointing of the Sick.

28.   Bishops alone can ordain men in the Sacrament of Holy Orders.

29. Bishops are the ordinary ministers of Confirmation although a priest can confirm in danger of death, at the time of adult Baptism or receiving an adult into the Church, and when given special delegation by the bishop.

30. All three (bishops, priests and deacons) are the ordinary ministers of Baptism and the ordinary official witnesses at the sacrament of Matrimony. They are also the ordinary ministers in the distribution of Eucharist.

31. All three can officially preach the homily at the liturgy.

Priesthood and the Unity of the Church

This linking of Holy Orders and Eucharist, and the requirement of hierarchical communion is the important foundation of the worldwide unit of the Catholic Church, as shown by the following:

a) The Pope alone can name someone a bishop.

b) The bishop alone can call a man to the priesthood or the diaconate.

c) Since only bishops and priests can bring about the Real Presence of Jesus in the Eucharist, the Catholic Church has an extremely strong bond of unity called hierarchical communion.

d) Throughout the world, priests must be in union with the bishop, and bishops must be in union with the Pope.

e) When the faithful celebrate Eucharist with their priest, they actually express a unique worldwide communion with all the Church.

32. Only the Holy Spirit bestows Church unity. However, a primary instrument of His unity is the Eucharist, Holy Orders, and hierarchical unity within the Church.

Holy Orders

Discipline of Celibacy

33. The New Testament witnesses to a new understanding in Jesus' Kingdom, namely, the value of virginity.

34. Jesus himself praises those who "have freely renounced sex for the sake of God's reign" (Mt. 19:12).

35. Paul writes, "The unmarried man is busy with the Lord's affairs, consumed with pleasing the Lord." (1Cor7:32) and "The virgin – indeed any unmarried woman – is concerned with things of the Lord, in pursuit of holiness in body and spirit." (7:34)

36. Under the Holy Spirit's inspiration, many Christians in the early centuries embraced virginity for the sake of the kingdom. At times, there were widespread movements. Thousands followed St. Anthony into the desert and great numbers followed St. Benedict into the monasteries.

37. Eventually, this spiritual impulse for virginity spread to those in Sacred Orders.

38. Often there were two groups of priests. Those who resided in the city with the bishop remained celibate. Those living alone in the rural areas married. This discipline of celibacy exists even today in many Eastern-rite Catholic churches.

Celibacy in the Latin Rite

39. During the first three or four centuries, no law was promulgated prohibiting clerical marriage. Celibacy was a matter of choice. However, a great number of clerics were unmarried.

40. The efforts of popes and regional councils began introducing celibacy as a legal requirement for receiving Holy Orders.

41. Over the centuries, the Church would experience a decline in the practice of celibacy (e.g. 10th and 15th century) which were followed by strong popes who restored the discipline.

42. The greatest restoration came at the Council of Trent (1563), which promulgated laws on celibacy, and encouraged the establishing of seminarians for priestly training (a task performed so well by St. Charles Borromeo).

43. Celibacy has always been a controversial aspect of priesthood. Arguments against this discipline focus on excellent men who would be priests if allowed to marry. Other arguments say that a married priesthood would be more credible and more in touch with the daily struggles of the Catholic people.

44. Celibacy for priests has two special gifts:
    a) Virginity is a sign of the presence of the kingdom.

b) "The unmarried man is busy with the Lord's affairs" (1Cor7:32)

45. The Catholic priesthood has been deeply embedded in the special gift of celibacy for so many centuries. In linking the two, priesthood and celibacy, the Church has heard a special call of the Spirit.